Autism and independence

A guide for local authorities: enabling adults
with an autism spectrum disorder to achieve
greater independence

Research by Edward Dowell

Compiled by Neil Johns and Annie Cooper, with contributions from Alan Bicknell,
Amanda Batten, Carol Povey, Mia Rosenblatt, Kathryn Quinton and Elizabeth Ayris

First published 2007 by The National Autistic Society
393 City Road, London EC1V 1NG
www.autism.org.uk

ISBN 978 1 905722 31 0

Designed by Column Communications

Printed by Crowes

Contents

Autism and independence

Autism and independence

Terminology

This report uses the abbreviation 'ASD' (autism spectrum disorder) to refer to all people with autism, including those with Asperger syndrome. However, where it refers to Asperger syndrome alone, the information given relates specifically to those who have been given this diagnosis.

Throughout this report, we refer to *Valuing people*, the Government's strategy for people with a learning disability, as many people with an ASD have an accompanying learning disability.

Autism and independence

Foreword

This report is about ordinary expectations and extraordinary people. In the course of interviewing people for this project – those with an autism spectrum disorder (ASD), service planners, commissioners, families – I was struck again and again by the 'ordinariness' of people's wishes: the desire for a place where they could enjoy living, the chance to pursue the things that matter to them, and an opportunity to obtain employment (whether economically gainful or not).

While more is now known about the nature of ASD, this understanding is not always reflected in government or local authority policies, local authority structures, commissioning strategies and services on the ground.

The Government has stated several key outcomes for adults towards which social care services should work, in order to improve people's quality of life:[1]

- improved health
- making a positive contribution
- exercise of choice and control
- freedom from discrimination and harassment
- economic well-being
- personal dignity.

This report aims to provide local authorities with helpful guidelines and recommendations which will support them in improving their services for adults with an ASD. Recognising the challenges facing local authorities, including commissioners and providers, the report also offers case studies of good practice alongside a series of key recommendations.

If this report can play even a small part in helping service planners and commissioners understand what they must do to make these outcomes a reality for more people with an ASD, it will have achieved its goal.

Edward Dowell

---

[1] Department of Health Green Paper (2005). *Independence, well-being and choice: our vision for the future of social care for adults in England.* London: Department of Health

Autism and independence

Executive summary

This report discusses how, through appropriate planning and service provision, people with an ASD can live their lives with as much independence as possible.

Key recommendations for local authorities

- Ensure that people with an ASD have access to a person-centred planning process.
- Ensure that commissioners, planners and senior managers, as well as frontline staff, receive ASD awareness training, so that they understand the uniqueness and complexity of ASD and the implications for service delivery.
- Use available data on children to inform the planning and commissioning of services for adults, including the future need for housing, so that services are available when these children leave school.
- Ensure that transition plans are in place for young people with an ASD from age 14 onwards.
- Develop protocols for joint working between learning disability and mental health teams, so that people with an ASD do not get passed between services.
- Create a joint forum in which housing departments, social services, local authority commissioners, health commissioners, health representatives, providers and user representatives can together plan services for adults with an ASD, including looking at joint finance. This forum could, for example, be an autism sub-group of the Learning Disability Partnership Board.
- Ensure that the model of housing provision offered to someone with an ASD meets their individual needs as outlined in their person-centred plan, and that a realistic assessment of the costs is made.
- Ensure that people with an ASD have access to flexible funding streams, including direct payments and individual budgets, and that there is adequate support to enable those who want to use them to do so.
- Ensure that adequate advocacy services with ASD-specific knowledge are available to those people who need them.

Local authority staff seeking further information on developing and running services for people with an ASD, or ASD awareness training, can contact The National Autistic Society (NAS). Visit www.autism.org.uk/la for details.

Autism and independence

Setting the scene

People with an ASD are among the most vulnerable and socially excluded in our society. Yet many adults with an ASD receive either no services or inadequate services and struggle to cope with everyday life.

Few have jobs (just 6% are in full-time paid employment[2]) and nearly half of all adults with an ASD live at home with their parents.

Many people with an ASD (especially those who have an IQ over 70) are frequently passed between learning disability and mental health teams at local authority level, with neither team accepting responsibility for assessment or providing services.

Despite many examples of good practice (some of them highlighted in this report), services that might enable people with an ASD to enjoy a more independent lifestyle are not widely available. These services should include advocacy and support with communication, budgeting and life skills, access to work and education, social and leisure activities, and a range of housing options, including support to maintain a tenancy.

This report is intended to help local authorities develop services that will lead to a greater measure of independence and choice for people with an ASD and a chance for their choices and aspirations to mean something.

Working with autism

Readers wanting a brief definition of ASD can find it on page 11. However, there is a growing recognition that an intellectual understanding of the 'triad of impairments' associated with an ASD (difficulties with social interaction, social communication and social imagination) is of limited use unless it is accompanied by an understanding of how ASD affects people's lives day by day. As one professional said:

> *"People need reminding of just how quirky the effects of ASD can be, and the flexibility and imagination that is needed to find solutions to people's needs."*

---

[2] Reid, B. (2007). *Moving on up? Negotiating the transition to adulthood for young people with autism.* London: The National Autistic Society. Available to download from www.autism.org.uk/transition

Autism and independence

Some professionals talk about the need to suspend the 'neurotypical' way of thinking in order to create services which respond to the individual needs of people with an ASD.

One of the recommendations of this report is that ASD awareness training is seen as important for commissioners, planners and senior managers, as well as for frontline staff, so that they understand the uniqueness and complexity of ASD, and also why services for people with an ASD are sometimes more expensive than those for people with, for example, learning disabilities.

It is impossible to underestimate the individuality of the effects of ASD. It can be said that no disability affects two people in quite the same way. But for ASD this is especially true.

Breaking glass
The parents of a young person with an ASD were alarmed when one morning their daughter started to systematically break windows in the family home. She couldn't explain why she was doing it, but the parents remembered the lyrics of a pop song their daughter liked at the time which referred to 'liking the sound of breaking glass'. The girl had interpreted it literally. Because her parents could see the connection, it helped them to enter into the world of their daughter and modify the behaviour – because they could see where it came from.

Sleeping on the sofa
After spending years in an institutional setting, Brian moved to a community-based service for people with an ASD where he had a self-contained flat within a larger service. Because Brian was used to institutional living it was difficult to persuade him to spend any time in his flat – he preferred the communal areas, even for sleeping. However, he did enjoy showers, so when a flat with a shower became empty staff offered Brian the chance to use it just for washing. After a while staff asked if he wanted a cup of tea in the flat, after his shower. Nearly a year later Brian asked to move to the flat full-time. Brian is now able to choose between spending his time on his own in his room, inviting people into his flat and going out to join others in the communal areas.

Understanding how an ASD can affect the details of someone's life is an essential step towards creating individual services to meet need. This demands a deeper understanding of ASD than is possible simply by knowing about the triad of impairments associated with the condition. However, it is useful for service providers to understand the main difficulties which all people with an ASD experience.

A brief description of ASD

ASD is a complex 'spectrum' disorder. People on the autism spectrum experience three main areas of difficulty, known as the triad of impairments.

- **Social interaction** – difficulty in social relationships, for example appearing aloof and indifferent to others.
- **Social communication** – difficulty with verbal and non-verbal communication, for example not fully understanding the meaning of common gestures, facial expressions or tone of voice.
- **Social imagination** – difficulty in the area of imagination and flexibility of thought, for example being interested in a limited range of activities which may be copied or pursued rigidly; difficulty with understanding what others think and feel.

In addition to the triad, people with an ASD may show a resistance to change and experience sensory sensitivity.

Many people with an ASD experience either hypersensitivity or hyposensitivity in at least one of the senses. Someone with heightened sensory sensitivity might find noise that other people would not notice intolerable, for example the noise from an electric light or a photocopier; another person might find that looking at certain patterns or colours on walls causes them distress. Meanwhile, someone with reduced sensory sensitivity might not respond quickly to pain, which could leave physical problems to persist or worsen.

People with a diagnosis of Asperger syndrome share the difficulties with social interaction, social communication and social imagination but generally have fewer problems with language, often speaking fluently. People with Asperger syndrome also often have average or above average intelligence.

More information about the complexity of ASDs is available on The National Autistic Society's website: www.autism.org.uk

How many people have an ASD?

The Medical Research Council (2001) estimates that ASD affects approximately 60 in 10,000 children under the age of eight. The most recent research available, by Baird et al, concluded that the prevalence of the disability is substantially higher than previously recognised, stating that children with an ASD constitute 1% of the child population.[3]

The NAS estimates that, overall, 1 in 100 people has an ASD. However, the precise number of adults with an ASD is not known. ASD assessment and diagnosis services for children have been improving in recent years, but before this, many people reached adulthood without receiving a diagnosis.

Today, many people do not receive a diagnosis of an ASD until they are adults (46% of adults with Asperger syndrome are diagnosed after the age of 16 according to one study[4]). At this stage, there are two factors affecting diagnosis statistics. Firstly, there is a shortage of diagnosticians across the UK who can assess and diagnose adults. Secondly, some adults may be in services where there are few incentives for an accurate diagnosis to be sought; others may have been misdiagnosed as having a mental health problem. There are undoubtedly many adults living with an ASD who have never been diagnosed and are completely unknown to service providers.

However, for those that are diagnosed, it is important that they are supported to live their lives with as much independence as possible. Equally, it is important to be aware of, and monitor, young people with an ASD to ensure that they make a smooth transition from children's services to adult life and achieve an appropriate degree of independence.

What is independence?

This report is designed to encourage local authorities to develop and commission services which enable people with an ASD to achieve a more independent way of life.

---

[3] Baird, G. et al (2006). Prevalence of disorders of the autistic spectrum in a population cohort of children in South Thames. *The Lancet*, 368, issue 9531, pp210-215

[4] The National Autistic Society (2001). *Ignored or ineligible? The reality for adults with an autistic spectrum disorder.* London: The National Autistic Society

The Disability Rights Commission defines independence as:

"All disabled people having the same choice, control and freedom as any other citizen – at home, at work and as members of the community. This does not necessarily mean 'doing everything for themselves', but it does mean that any practical assistance people need should be based on their own choices and aspirations."

Independence can mean very different things to different people, depending on their level of need. For one person it might mean eventually buying their own home, for another it might mean deciding what to wear.

The relationship between independence and choice should be made clear. Choice should not be seen as simply a means of achieving an independent lifestyle. For many people, exercising choice **will** mean moving to a more independent way of life. But for others it will mean **choosing a more supported way of life**. In exercising the choice **not** to live independently, people can be gaining increased independence of choice.

Whatever the level of eventual independence, it cannot be achieved in a single step. It requires a combination of practical services which come together to enable someone to achieve a more independent lifestyle. This can include, for example:

- how services are planned and delivered (person-centred planning and transition planning)
- where someone lives (housing)
- how someone spends their day (employment or purposeful activity)
- opportunities for social and leisure activities
- relationships (who people choose to spend time with)
- advocacy (to enable people's views to be heard).

All of the above need to be underpinned by adequate, flexible resources; together they form the basis on which an independent life can be built.

Independence can be fostered both by the attitudes of the people supporting the person with an ASD, as well as by the physical environment within which the support is offered.

Service providers and local authorities play a vital role in helping people to become more independent. Although independence will 'look' very different to different people, there are nonetheless clear outcomes which statutory services should strive to achieve. *Valuing people*, the Government's plan to improve services for people with learning disabilities, states that promoting independence is one of its key aims.

"While people's individual needs will differ, the starting presumption should be one of independence rather than dependence, with public services providing the support needed to maximise this."

The reality now

Research conducted by The National Autistic Society shows that most people with an ASD are simply not receiving the support that could enable them to enjoy independent living.

As a result, very few have jobs, live in their own homes or have choice over who cares for them.

- 44% of adults aged 25 and over are still living at home. Of those adults living away from their family, only 4% are living fully independently and 30% are living semi-independently in some form of supported housing.[5]
- Only 9% of people are receiving social skills training.[6]
- Only 15% of adults are in full-time paid employment.[7]
- A quarter (24%) of adults with an ASD are doing nothing at all or just 'helping out around the house'.[8]
- Only 11% of carers stated that the adult they cared for had ever used an independent advocate.[9]
- Only 38% of people with an ASD have a community care assessment. Only 16% of people with an ASD were actually offered one in the first place; others have to ask or fight for one.[10]
- Only 53% of young adults have a transition plan in place.[11]

[5] Broach, S. et al (2003). *Autism: rights in reality*. London: The National Autistic Society. Available to download from www.autism.org.uk/rightsinreality

[6] Broach, S. et al (2003). *Autism: rights in reality*. London: The National Autistic Society

[7] Reid, B. (2007). *Moving on up? Negotiating the transition to adulthood for young people with autism.* London: The National Autistic Society

[8] The National Autistic Society (2001). *Ignored or ineligible? The reality for adults with an autistic spectrum disorder.*

[9] Broach, S. et al (2003). *Autism: rights in reality*. London: The National Autistic Society

[10] The National Autistic Society (2001). *Ignored or ineligible? The reality for adults with an autistic spectrum disorder.* London: The National Autistic Society

[11] The National Autistic Society (2006). *make school make sense. Autism and education: the reality for families today.* London: The National Autistic Society

While there may be general agreement that people with an ASD should be able to enjoy independent living, in reality there is clearly a very long way to go to achieve this.

The responsibilities of the statutory authorities

Amongst statutory agencies there is a long-standing confusion about whether services for people with an ASD fall within the responsibility of learning disability or mental health teams. The result is that all too frequently it is neither.

For those people with an ASD who have an IQ of less than 70 the situation is relatively straightforward – they fall within the remit of learning disability services.[12]

But for people at the medium or higher-functioning end of the spectrum (typically with a higher IQ) the situation is more complex, since they may be regarded as having neither a learning disability nor a mental illness. The result is that neither learning disability nor mental health teams take responsibility for assessment and service provision, and many people with an ASD simply fall through the gaps in the system.

It should be noted that, in the absence of assessment and services, many people with an ASD go on to develop mental health problems – such as depression, nervous breakdown or suicidal feelings – and sometimes end up in acute psychiatric wards or prison. More timely support could often have prevented this happening.

> *"Mental health and learning disability units spent three months trying to decide who was responsible for my son – meanwhile his condition got worse."*
> **Parent, Bristol**

In November 2006, the Department of Health issued *Better services for people with an autistic spectrum disorder: a note clarifying current government policy and describing good practice*.[13] This looks at existing Government policy and clarifies how it applies to adults with an ASD. The policies covered are:

- *Fair access to care*
- *Valuing people*

---

[12] The number of people with an ASD who have an additional learning disability is not known as there is no central register of people with an ASD.

[13] Department of Health (2006). *Better services for people with an autistic spectrum disorder: a note clarifying current government policy and describing good practice*. London: Department of Health

- *Our health, our care, our say*
- *Improving the life chances of disabled people*
- National service framework for mental health
- National service framework for long-term (neurological) conditions.

Key implementation issues for local areas cover responsibility and funding; commissioning; assessment and review; monitoring and regulation; service provision; community integration, and transition. One issue covered is the problem of people with an ASD falling through the gaps created by traditional service boundaries, and the document states that 'the current position whereby some people with an ASD 'fall through' local services – in particular between mental health and learning disability services – is unacceptable and contrary to the intention of Government policy.' The document goes on to say that individual assessments should be the starting point for getting people the services they need. These services may come from more than one local authority team, working in partnership with each other, if this best supports the individual.

Research also shows that parents are confused by which statutory agency is responsible for their son's or daughter's welfare. 59% agreed that responsibility for funding and providing care and support fell between two agencies. Two thirds (66%) of those whose child had a community care assessment said that there was no lead agency responsible for their son or daughter.[14]

Often it is less important which service takes responsibility – whether learning disability, vulnerable adults or mental health teams. What matters is that **someone** takes the lead for assessing need and that there is a clear protocol in place. It is also important that different teams can work together successfully, if necessary, to support identified needs.

> *"I wish they would make up their minds what I am."*
> **Person with an ASD**

Policy context

Local authorities are operating within a rapidly changing policy environment. There is not room in this document to expand on all legislation and Government policy relevant to people with an ASD, but it includes:

---

[14] The National Autistic Society (2001). *Ignored or ineligible? The reality for adults with an autistic spectrum disorder.* London: The National Autistic Society

- *Disability Discrimination Act 1995*
- *Disability Discrimination Act 2005*
- *NHS and Community Care Act 1990* – giving people a legal right to an assessment (though not necessarily to services)
- *Fair access to care: guidance to eligibility criteria for adult social care* (Department of Health, 2003)
- *Carers (Recognition and Services) Act 1995*
- *Carers (Equal Opportunities) Act 2005*
- *Valuing people: a new strategy for learning disability for the 21st century* (Department of Health, 2001)
- *Supporting people* initiative 2003.

The White Paper from the Department of Health[15], *Our health, our care, our say*, also seeks to define the responsibilities of local authorities for social care, including recommending the use of direct payments and individual budgets to provide flexible care and support.

ASD and *Valuing people*

Some people with an ASD are being excluded from the benefits of *Valuing people*, the Government's strategy for people with a learning disability.[16]

Valuing people only applies to people with an ASD if they also have a learning disability. The definition of learning disability in *Valuing people* includes the presence of:

- a significantly reduced ability to understand new or complex information, to learn new skills (impaired intelligence)
- a reduced ability to cope independently (impaired social functioning) which started before adulthood, with a lasting effect on development.

Arguably, this definition is wide enough to apply to some people with Asperger syndrome or high-functioning autism.

---

[15] Department of Health (2006). *Our health, our care, our say*. London: Department of Health

[16] Department of Health (2001). *Valuing people: a new strategy for learning disability for the 21st century*. London: Department of Health

Guidance in *Valuing people* states that 'adults with Asperger's syndrome or higher-functioning autism are not precluded from using learning disability services, and may, where appropriate, require an assessment of their social functioning and social skills in order to establish their level of need'.[17]

Local authorities should therefore take the opportunity to include people with an ASD who have an IQ over 70 in *Valuing people* initiatives with services designed to meet their needs.

In reality, however, this has yet to become accepted practice. The result is that people with an ASD often fail to benefit from advances in services brought about by *Valuing people*. For example, people with an ASD are least likely to receive a person-centred plan, one of the cornerstones of *Valuing people*.[18]

Guidance to directors of adult social services

Local authorities should ensure that they implement recent guidance to directors of adult social services (DASS).[19] This guidance requires directors to make it clear which team or manager should be assessing and meeting the eligible needs of a range of client groups. ASD is specifically mentioned as one of the client groups. The reality is, though, that many people with Asperger syndrome and high-functioning autism continue to be passed between mental health and learning disability teams, with neither accepting responsibility for assessment or providing services.

In the following chapters we will look at how local authorities, commissioners and providers can work together to develop services for people with an ASD and support greater independence of choice.

---

[17] Department of Health (2001). *Implementing valuing people: a new strategy for learning disability for the 21st century*. London: Department of Health

[18] Institute of Health Research, Lancaster University (2005). *Impact of person-centred planning*. Lancaster: Lancaster University

[19] Department of Health (2006). *Guidance on the statutory chief officer post of the director of adult social services* and *Best practice guidance on the role of director of adult social services*. London: Department of Health

Commissioning

Does the local authority know about the adults with an ASD living in its area: who they are and what opportunities and support they need?

The provision of services for people with an ASD presents commissioners across the country with a huge challenge. This section outlines some of the approaches to commissioning that are most likely to result in the individual needs of people with an ASD being met.

The number of children and adults being diagnosed with an ASD has grown considerably in recent years. Applying the most recent estimate of prevalence to the population as a whole means that an average local authority with a population of 250,000 could have around 2,500 people with an ASD within its borders.[20]

Services need to be built around individual needs, rather than assuming that what suits one person will also suit another. While this is true for all people, the diversity and individuality of ASD means that no two people will be affected in quite the same way (even if their 'level' of disability is roughly the same).

Traditional types of residential and day services are being replaced by more individual services, such as supported living or outreach support and flexible funding arrangements. This requires a different role for commissioners, with a much greater emphasis on person-centred planning, flexibility, joint funding and partnerships with providers.

All involved realise that commissioning is about using best value to decide how to allocate resources to achieve maximum impact. Often a small amount of money provided early on can prevent more intensive and expensive services being needed at a later stage.

Understanding needs

It is only possible to provide person-centred commissioning through an understanding of the effect of an ASD on an individual's daily life. As discussed in the

[20] Baird, G. et al (2006). Prevalence of disorders of the autistic spectrum in a population cohort of children in South Thames. *The Lancet*, 368, issue 9531, pp210-215

previous chapter, this requires more than just basic awareness training in ASD. Care managers and commissioners should attend ASD training events alongside frontline staff to understand how the condition impacts on service design and delivery.

Planning services

Commissioners will need to conduct an audit of services for people with an ASD in order to determine whether existing services are sufficient to meet need both now and in the future. Indeed, services often need to be commissioned several years in advance to meet the needs of young people with an ASD. This can only be achieved if local authority commissioners know about them. Commissioners should therefore work closely with children's services to share information on the number of young people with an ASD in the local area and their likely support needs to help plan appropriate services.

This should include ensuring that information available through integrated children's systems is appropriately shared with all relevant decision makers and is used to inform future planning and commissioning of adult services, too. In addition, data gathered by the existing school census, which already shows the number of children with a statement and on School Action Plus, should inform the planning and commissioning of services for adults, so that services are available when these children leave school. However, this data does not provide a complete picture as it will not include children excluded from the school system, those who are being home-educated or those who are not receiving support through School Action Plus or a statement. It will also depend on the awareness of school staff, as teachers record primary need.

Autism team shares database with LEA

In South Staffordshire, members of the autism special placement team meet regularly with local authority staff to plan services for children with complex needs from Year 9 (age 14) identified through the local authority's database. Transition meetings are then held with a multi-disciplinary team which includes representatives from education and social services. The aim is to identify services that might be needed in five years' time, so that commissioners have time to plan services. By planning in advance, commissioners also hope to reduce the number of out-of-county placements, by making sure appropriate services are available locally.

Commissioners should also ensure that the details contained in all the different person-centred plans are brought together to inform an overall commissioning strategy, so that identified needs are met.

Rob Greig, National Director, *Valuing people*, says: 'The information from people's person-centred plans should be the starting point for all service planning and commissioning decisions.'

The Foundation for People with Learning Difficulties has created a tool, *Shaping the future together*[21], designed to assist in this process.

Clarity over responsibility for adults with an ASD

There should be a clear understanding of which local authority team will take the lead in identifying services needed by people with an ASD, including people with Asperger syndrome, who are not currently regarded as qualifying for a service from either the learning disability or mental health teams.[22] Recent guidance issued to directors of adult social services by the Department of Health states that they should be clear which team or manager is assessing and meeting the needs of people with an ASD.

Newham co-ordinates services for people with high-functioning autism
Newham Adult Services, in partnership with ELCMHT (East London and The City Mental Health Trust), have launched a project to co-ordinate the delivery of services for adults with Asperger syndrome or high-functioning autism.

An initial report from the partnership found that people who receive a diagnosis of Asperger syndrome or high-functioning autism were generally receiving ineffective and costly services, such as crisis management, because there were no specific services for this group.

Demographics for Newham suggest that over 650 adults would meet the diagnostic criteria, however, only a small number are known to services. In developing a service, Newham will enable those people to access appropriate support. The new service aims to:

[21] Foundation for People with Learning Difficulties (2005). *Shaping the future together*. London: Foundation for People with Learning Difficulties

[22] Powell, A. (2002). *Taking responsibility: good practice guidelines for services – adults with Asperger syndrome*. London: The National Autistic Society

- provide easier access to assessment
- provide individual assessments to those who meet the criteria to determine the impact of Asperger syndrome or high-functioning autism
- signpost to provider agencies, services and advice
- provide a specialist service to support the most complex needs of some individuals.

The project also offers training to partnership agencies, including colleges, voluntary groups and community groups to raise awareness of Asperger syndrome and high-functioning autism. It aims to improve the accessibility of community services to adults who have Asperger syndrome or high-functioning autism, which will hopefully include education and employment opportunities.

The project plans ongoing development work with involvement from service users and carers and will be consulting on a long-term strategy to ensure that the needs of this group are properly recognised and supported.

Partnerships are an integral part of the way the independent and voluntary sector works in Newham. There has been close consultation with The National Autistic Society throughout.

Joint working

Meeting the needs of people with an ASD requires a partnership between health, social services and housing authorities – and between the statutory, voluntary and independent sectors.

Commissioning can be done collaboratively, with several local authorities working together to pool information and approaches. The Greater Manchester consortium is a good example of how local authorities can work together to enhance local services for adults with autism.

Ten local authorities pool resources to plan autism services
Ten social services departments in the Greater Manchester area have been working together since 1997 to identify the needs of local people with an ASD and plan services to meet them.

They have collated statistics of people known to services, services already available and the costs of out-of-area placements. They meet regularly to share good practice and develop a collective regional strategy.

As well as jointly funding a development officer employed by The National Autistic Society, consortium members have developed new services, such as befriending schemes, and several members are now seeking formal autism accreditation [see the section on accreditation on page 28] for their general learning disability services. They are also starting to look at the joint commissioning of short break respite services.

The ten councils are Bolton, Bury, Manchester, Oldham, Rochdale, Salford, Stockport, Tameside, Trafford and Wigan. Following the success of this model a similar consortium has been developed in the North East too, supported by The National Autistic Society.

Working with providers

Most commissioners now operate provider forums – opportunities for commissioners and providers to get together to share information and ideas. Commissioners can give providers a clear idea of commissioning priorities (including how they are interpreting relevant legislation and guidance), while providers can respond with ideas of how best to meet the commissioners' needs, as well as feeding back up-to-date information and their development plans. As one provider says:

> "The forums work best if you feel you are in a meeting with people who can influence decision-making. It's a chance for us to keep up-to-date with their strategy and policy so we can see how we fit into their wider picture."

Commissioners should make sure that senior managers attend all provider forum meetings and that a good cross-section of providers is invited to attend.

Notes from all provider forum meetings should be fed into authorities' Learning Disability Partnership Boards, which all local authorities are required to have under the Government's *Valuing people* strategy, so that they inform the decision-making process of these bodies.

User involvement

The *Disability Discrimination Act 2005* places a new duty on public bodies to promote equality of opportunity for disabled people: the Disability Equality Duty. This means that local authorities have to involve disabled people in a wide range of functions. Commissioners and planners should take advantage of this opportunity to ensure that they involve people with an ASD.

It is vital that people with an ASD and/or those acting on their behalf are represented on local authority Learning Disability Partnership Boards. This will help to ensure that the specific and different needs and views of people with an ASD are not overlooked in general discussions about learning disability. Ideally, each board should have an ASD sub-group (also attended by commissioners) focusing specifically on these issues.

Some local authorities now run consultation days at which users can meet with commissioners and providers.

Surrey autism project

In 2005, Surrey County Council employed an autism project manager to focus on a group of 42 young people with an ASD aged between 14 and 25 years old. They set up a social evening for carers, as well as a conference geared at people with an ASD and at professionals. A range of initiatives has been established following this piece of work, including a network of 'autism champions' from across the county, a social group for people with Asperger syndrome, and person-centred housing options plans for ten young people.

Provision of advocacy services

Improving advocacy services is another way to get a better understanding of people's wishes and needs. Because of the communication difficulties people with an ASD experience, access to advocacy can be critical in ensuring that people are able to express their aspirations, interpret and process information regarding their rights and request relevant services. Advocacy support can be particularly useful during the transition to adulthood and adult services; in accessing housing; in accessing employment; to provide assistance with social integration and life planning; and in accessing health services.

At present many people with an ASD find it hard to access advocacy – only 11% of carers stated that the adult they cared for had ever used an independent advocate.[23] Local authorities should ensure not only that people with an ASD are able to access advocacy services but that advocacy services are trained to support people with an ASD.

Advocacy for autism and Asperger syndrome

Speakeasy Advocacy has been providing advocacy for people with learning disabilities in Basingstoke since 1993, but soon began to focus on autism and Asperger syndrome. Two self-advocacy groups specifically for people with Asperger syndrome were established in the late 1990s and are still going strong today.

People coming to the groups can get one-to-one support when they want to access services, uphold their rights or get information. This is crucial for people with Asperger syndrome, as they often find it difficult to access any support because of the gap between learning disability and mental health services. In Speakeasy's experience, advocacy is often the only way to prevent or end social exclusion.

People can also meet with their peers to develop confidence and self-advocacy skills in a social setting where there is less pressure to 'fit in'.

The key has been empowering members to take control of their own lives through their advocacy relationships and self-advocacy groups. All staff and volunteers in our project have an awareness of autism and Asperger syndrome, but members are encouraged to tell staff what they want, as they are all individuals with their own needs. Staff are more tolerant of certain behaviours than other services and don't judge, but instead support people to behave appropriately in an empowering way by explaining choices and consequences.

Relationships are built up over time and a great deal of patience is necessary as many group members mistrust other professionals, or even their own families. Many members now feel able to call in and speak in confidence with anyone at the project, regardless of whether they are their named advocate.

23 Broach, S. et al (2003). *Autism: rights in reality*. London: The National Autistic Society

Involving people with Asperger syndrome in the development of the service has definitely helped it give the right advocacy support to people. Another key ingredient has been self-advocacy, as people are able to become more independent through learning from, and developing skills with, their peers. Demand for the service continues to rise, suggesting that advocacy is essential for people with autism and Asperger syndrome now more than ever.

The *Mental Capacity Act 2005* created a new statutory service, the Independent Mental Capacity Advocate (IMCA) Service. NHS bodies and local authorities have to instruct and consult the IMCA in important decisions about serious medical treatment or change of residence for people who have no family or friends.

ASD-specific design

Because of the nature of ASDs and the inherent difficulties people have with social interaction and sensory sensitivity, the following issues need to be considered when commissioning housing and support services.

- Buildings need to be creatively designed to take into account people's need for a low arousal environment, for example they may have more space and larger corridors. (This can result in higher building costs than for other types of learning disability services.)
- Where services are delivered from non purpose-built properties the buildings may need to be adapted to take into account the needs of people with an ASD.
- ASD-specific services may need a higher level of staff compared to other learning disability services, in order to support some challenging or complex behaviours and offer a service which responds to individual needs.
- Staff will require ASD-specific training and ongoing professional development.
- SMART technology can enable greater independence (see the case study on provision in Newport, opposite).

Two case studies from NAS services show how good design and staff training can benefit service users.

Getting the environment right

In partnership with a local housing association, The National Autistic Society in Newport has designed a new ASD-specific service for six young people in their early 20s with very complex behaviour and high support needs.

Initial outlay was higher than average due to large capital start-up costs entailed in the purpose-built self-contained flats and the staffing and training expenses attached to the project. The flats needed to be robust, with heavy doors and hinges, yet spacious, airy and light with high ceilings and wide corridors to avoid the feelings of claustrophobia that many people with an ASD experience. Triple glazed windows and integral blinds were included to keep the flats soundproof. Assistive technology enables tenants to remain secure and independent in their own flats and staff are able to communicate effectively with one another, and also to provide support and intervention as and when required, minimising risk. This innovative service is to be evaluated by the Special Projects Team from Bro Morgannwg NHS Trust.

Would you like to go out?

Because of the nature of ASD it might take someone an hour or more to decide whether or not they would like to do a particular activity, such as go for a walk.[24] If someone takes a long time to decide that, yes, they would like to go for a walk, only to be told that it's now too late, it can set up a negative pattern of behaviour. An autism-specific service will therefore need staff in place to respond to people's expressed wishes **whenever they express them**. This is likely to mean a higher ratio of staff to users compared to a general learning disability service and ASD-specific staff training.

Designing services with people with an ASD in mind can result in high initial costs, but there are benefits in the long term. This needs to be taken into account when deciding which services are likely to offer best value.

---

[24] People with an ASD may need time to process all the implications behind a simple question such as 'Would you like to go for a walk?' What's the weather like? Do I need a coat? If I take a coat and I get too hot, what happens to the coat? How long should I walk? Where should I go? Will I meet that person I don't like? Reaching a decision may therefore be a long process.

Preventative action

There is a natural tendency to focus resources on people with a higher level of support needs (ie those who are most vulnerable). However, *Fair access to care*, published by the Department of Health, states that local authorities should 'identify needs that will worsen for the lack of timely help'.[25] This acknowledges that relatively small amounts of money spent at the right time on appropriate support can play a real part in preventing higher-level needs arising later on. The White Paper *Our health, our care, our say* also recognised the importance of preventative services, and this was one of the major focuses of the document.

Harrow Asperger group

Each month adults with Asperger syndrome in Harrow come along to a group run by The National Autistic Society's Harrow Branch, where they can meet and talk about issues on their mind, supported by a trained counsellor. Topics discussed include coping with social situations, relationships and sexuality, anger management and depression. Having a trained counsellor on hand (funded by the local authority) means people are offered low-level professional support with their anxieties and issues, which might otherwise escalate into more serious situations. The group meets for two hours once a month.

Glasgow Autism Resource Centre

Adults with an ASD living in the Greater Glasgow area can use a drop-in facility at the city's Autism Resource Centre, a one-stop shop offering information, assessment and post-diagnostic support. The service is jointly funded by the health board, city council and local voluntary organisations. Post-diagnostic support groups are offered in areas such as social development, leisure, art, creative writing and photography – a chance for adults with an ASD to meet others and receive low-level, ongoing support.

Accreditation

Autism-specific services can seek accreditation from one of the recognised assessing bodies, such as Autism Accreditation of The National Autistic Society (see www.autism.org.uk/accreditation) or the British Institute for Learning Disabilities (BILD). General learning disability services can also consider seeking accreditation if they offer services to people with an ASD.

---

[25] Department of Health (2003). *Fair access to care services: guidance on eligibility criteria for adult social care.* London: Department of Health

Autism accreditation signifies that a service has a specialised knowledge of ASDs which is used to inform all aspects of its practice, management and allocation of resources. It is a quality assurance programme. It also allows accredited organisations to share good practice.

The benefits of accreditation

In Oldham's Adult Learning Disability Service, gaining autism accreditation – initially for its supported living service – was successful because of the input of a member of staff with a remit for accreditation issues, as well as the support and guidance of The National Autistic Society's Autism Accreditation adviser and the commitment of other key personnel in the service. Once this had been achieved, the benefits of the whole process were seen to be so great that the organisation decided to work to an extension of its accreditation. In 2006, its respite services gained accreditation and its day services are currently working through the process.

Significantly, accreditation has brought about a cultural change in the organisation: staff teams have become more structured and they work together more coherently. The staff training which took place as a result of the accreditation process also had a major effect: skill levels have increased, as has staff motivation and confidence. Improved communication with service users has resulted in a decrease in behavioural issues. The need for out-of-borough placements has also decreased.

Key recommendations for local authorities

- Make sure that commissioners receive autism awareness training on how ASD impacts on people's lives, so that they understand how their decisions affect the lives of people with an ASD.
- Use information from integrated children's systems and the school census to assist planning adult services later on.
- Ensure that people with Asperger syndrome and high-functioning autism who need assessment and services do not get passed around between mental health and learning disability teams.
- Ensure that people with an ASD are included in the action taken by the local authority to meet the requirements of the Disability Equality Duty.
- Set up an autism sub-group of the Learning Disability Partnership Board so that the particular needs of people with an ASD are considered in this forum.

- Be realistic about the cost of ASD-specific services and the reasons why they are often more expensive than general learning disability services.
- Ensure that preventative services are provided as well as more intensive services for people with complex needs.
- Ensure that ASD-specific services are accredited by a recognised agency, and consider seeking accreditation for general learning disability services if they work with people with an ASD.

Transition to adult life

Is the local authority anticipating the long-term needs of children with an ASD currently in the school system and enabling young people to make the transition to a more independent, adult life after school?

Transition can be a particularly difficult time for young people with autism, as they can find change very difficult. They can also find it difficult to visualise, or to consider, events beyond their daily routine, for example what they would like to do in the future. Without adequate preparation, changes in the environment or routines can lead to high levels of anxiety and, possibly, to the failure of the transition. For these reasons, effective and timely planning for transition is essential.

The transition process is an opportunity to build a detailed picture of the support someone needs to build their learning and skills so that they are better placed to make a successful transition from school to adult life. It should be a flexible framework around which different organisations and individuals can converge. Taking a person-centred approach to the transition process means that an individual's hopes, aspirations and ambitions are more likely to be achieved.

Planning for transition from children's to adult services should start at around the time an individual reaches 14 years of age (although, ideally, preparation would begin much sooner) and may last until they are 25 years old (see the timeline on page 32). For young people with a statement of special educational needs, the *Special educational needs code of practice* [26] outlines that transition planning should start at the annual review meeting when a young person reaches 14. This should not just focus on education, but should include all agencies that may be involved in planning for the person's future, as set out in the national service framework for children, young people and maternity services.[27]

---

[26] Department for Education and Skills (2002). *Special educational needs code of practice*. London: Department for Education and Skills

[27] Department of Health and Department for Education and Skills (2004). *National service framework for children, young people and maternity services*. London: Department of Health

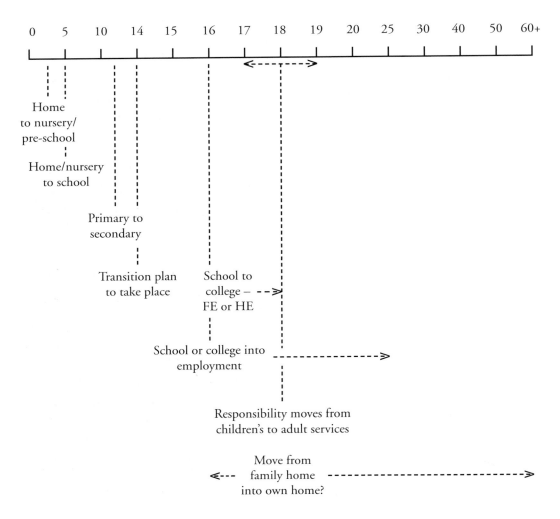

Timeline: planning for transition from children's to adult services

This section explores some of the factors which can help to reduce that uncertainty for people with an ASD around transition, and support a successful move into adult life.

Transition planning

Transition planning is essential in order to describe the needs of an individual and put support in place to meet those needs as people move from school to adult life.

If transition fails, young people can find themselves embedded more firmly than ever in the family home, increasing stress on the family and resulting in more isolated lives.

Getting the support right

For Lucy, a 19-year-old with an ASD, transition into mainstream further education did not initially go well. She demonstrated her distress at college through urinary incontinence on an almost daily basis, and in her behaviour, for example stealing food from the college and spilling drinks over herself and other students.

Her college contacted the NAS Leicestershire outreach team because it felt it did not have the resources or training to provide the right support for Lucy, who was attending one of its learning disability courses. Staff felt that they did not understand Lucy's behaviours.

The NAS used a 'triad assessment tool' to assess how Lucy's ASD affected her in the areas of social imagination, interaction and communication and found that she experienced significant difficulties.

After working with Lucy and in consultation with her parents and the college, Lucy was provided with a portable communication system – a pictorial schedule showing the structure of her day at college – and general guidelines for working with Lucy were written.

Following these changes Lucy suffered no further episodes of incontinence and her changed behaviour indicated that she was more settled in college.

This case study shows how appropriate intervention can help a young person with an ASD to make a successful transition from school to adult life.

The local authority's responsibilities

At the same time as planning the transition of each individual, it is critical that the local authority has a clear idea of the **overall** number of children and young people with an ASD who are likely to need services and support once they leave school. The key questions for local authorities to ask themselves are:

- do we know how many young people with an ASD will be leaving school in three to five years' time and requiring support?
- do we have a picture of the type of support or services they will need?
- are commissioning decisions being made now to make sure that support is available locally in three to five years' time?
- if a young person, who may already be approaching a transition period, is diagnosed with an ASD, do we have the capacity to meet their needs?

Social services often have little idea of the high numbers of young people with an ASD coming through the education system at present. Local authorities should know the number of children in the system, be tracking each one as they progress through children's services, and using this information as a planning tool.

Planning for the future in Surrey

Surrey County Council has commissioned a report into how services for people with an ASD in the county can be made more responsive and effective.

The county's Autism Group gathered information from young people between the ages of 14 and 25 who are in transition, their carers and professionals who work with them. Its findings were used to decide what services need to be planned and developed for adults with an ASD.

The project report – *What I want is* – concluded that there is an urgent need to develop a wider ranging service with a specialist understanding of people with an ASD across the county. Services need to be flexible and person-centred.

The report was also able to make predictions about the growing number of people with an ASD and develop a plan for action. It is hoped that accurate planning will avoid crisis responses and inappropriate and expensive out-of-county placements.

Many different agencies should be involved in supporting a young person to make the transition to adult life, including schools, local authorities, the Connexions service, social services, housing providers, further and higher education providers and employers.

At present, however, post-school transition all too often consists of social workers trying to find a placement or services when the young person is just a few months away from leaving school. This leaves little time for a young person and their family to make real choices about the options available to them, or to manage the transition to a new environment in small stages. Clearly this 'last-minute' approach is also likely to result in people being matched to services on the basis of availability rather than because that service is best suited to their individual needs.

While the local authority does not have sole responsibility for ensuring successful transition, where transition fails, it is likely that the local authority social services department will be asked to intervene in a crisis situation.

Last-minute placements cause problems

Nineteen-year-old Christopher was excited about moving from Sunfield – a school in Worcestershire which provides education and residential care for children with severe learning disabilities and ASDs – into a new supported living arrangement close to his family home.

Sunfield forwarded detailed information about Christopher to his new care provider but was concerned about the shortage of time allowed for finding him accommodation. Despite assurances to the contrary, when Christopher arrived at his new home it was not ready. Staff were still assembling beds and wardrobes and the washing machine, fridge and freezer remained in boxes in the kitchen.

To make matters worse the member of staff who had been given responsibility for getting to know Christopher announced that she would be leaving her job within a couple of days.

Two weeks later Christopher was reported to be in 'a terrible state' and staff caring for him were considering having him detained under the *Mental Health Act*. This was avoided and Christopher was admitted to an assessment centre where he stayed for five months. He has now been found a supported living service and things are going well. But his family say they have lost confidence in anyone being able to care adequately for Christopher following his initial 'disastrous' transition.

The importance of planning ahead

The only way to avoid a last-minute approach is to plan ahead, understand the level of need and create services to match at an early stage.

If a Learning Disability Partnership Board has an autism sub-group then this may well be the best channel for identifying needs and thinking through the future implications for services such as housing, transport and leisure. This will involve their working closely with a wide range of partners including health authorities, housing departments, the Learning and Skills Council, social services, the voluntary sector and independent providers.

Every Learning Disability Partnership Board should have a transition champion – someone who is making sure that the needs of people with an ASD during transition are being considered by all relevant professionals.

Autism and independence

Local authorities should take a leading role in co-ordinating and preparing for transitions. This could include forming a transition planning group specifically for people with an ASD and including all professionals relevant to transition planning from school to adult life, such as:

- learning support representatives from each local further education college (or similar)
- local university disability officer (or similar)
- senior SENCO representative from the local secondary school SENCO network
- senior educational psychologist
- Connexions personal adviser for complex needs in mainstream schools
- social services representatives
- voluntary sector representatives.

The multi-agency approach

Nottingham City Council is setting up a multi-agency transition team that will operate on two tiers.

A steering group of strategic managers from Connexions and the council's education, social services and health departments has recently given the go-ahead to the initiative, with the aim of encouraging agencies to work together more cohesively and effectively.

A working group run by a project manager seconded from social services, and which includes a Connexions personal adviser, a transition co-ordinator from social services, a transition nurse and an educational psychologist, will work with a social worker and an education administrator to provide specialist transition support to more young people.

Young people from state and specialist schools who are statemented or who are on School Action and School Action Plus will have their cases reviewed. This means that young people who might previously have missed out on the transition procedure, such as those with Asperger syndrome, will now be included.

The focus of the initiative will be on common assessment and policy procedures for transition, development of multi-agency teams and the incorporation of person-centred planning.

Cambridgeshire Learning and Skills Council

Cambridgeshire Learning and Skills Council (LSC) wants to improve its services for young people with an ASD by working more closely with associated agencies at local level.

Through inclusion to excellence, a recent strategic review of planning and funding of LSC provision for learners with disabilities, identified a need for the LSC to work in the local community 'to ensure learning is of high quality, learner-centred and cost effective'.

With national funding Cambridgeshire LSC set up a course at Huntingdonshire Regional College. The course was designed for a group of young people with ASDs from a local specialist school who would otherwise have had little choice but to continue their education at a specialist residential college out of county.

The LSC worked closely with Connexions and other key agencies to develop a flexible learning package for each student. The college has developed strong links with the local specialist school to make sure transition is as seamless as possible and has arrangements with a number of external collaborative partners delivering a range of courses.

There are plans to roll out this pilot, part of an Eastern Counties Pathfinder initiative, to other areas.

The role of Connexions

The formal transition process for a child with a statement begins with a transition review when the child is 14, in Year 9.

The Connexions service – the advice and guidance service for all 13-19 year olds – has particular responsibilities for young people with special educational needs (SEN). Where a young person has a statement, the relevant Connexions personal adviser must attend the Year 9 annual review and the service is responsible for overseeing implementation of the transition plan for that young person, which is drawn up following the review.

For young people with statements, Connexions is also under a duty to arrange assessments of the young person's needs and the provision required to meet those needs post-16. This may include access to continuing education, occupational training or employment.

However, many children with an ASD do not have statements and are therefore not entitled to a transition review at 14. If they need social support their parents can request a social services assessment of need under section 17 of the *Children Act 1989*. Connexions personal advisers can also decide if the young person requires support under the *Learning and Skills Act 2000*, section 140. This allows for an assessment of need to take place before the person leaves school, and could cover social support needs.

Since Connexions has such a key role in transition, it is vital that all Connexions personal advisers working with young people with an ASD have a good understanding of ASD and its impact.

The Government has stated its intention to devolve responsibility for commissioning Information, Advice and Guidance (IAG), and the funding that goes with it, from Connexions to local authorities.[28] Children's trusts are being established in each local authority area and the funding that currently goes to the 47 Connexions partnerships will go directly to each of the 150 local authority areas by April 2008. The needs of young people with an ASD must be met under the new structures.

Government guidance on transition

The Department for Education and Skills published detailed guidelines[29] to help statutory services facilitate the transition process for children with an ASD. These indicate key pointers for local authorities, Connexions and others involved in transition. For example:

- does the LEA have policies and procedures for the transition of children with an ASD from school to post-school provision?
- are there adequate record-keeping and profiling methods to allow information to accompany the children with an ASD when they move on?
- is there good preparation for transfer to college or other post-16 provision?
- are Connexions personal advisers aware of the needs of clients with an ASD and their families and the available suitable provision?

---

[28] Department for Education and Skills (2006). *Youth matters: next steps.* London: Department for Education and Skills

[29] Department for Education and Skills (2002). *Autistic spectrum disorders: good practice guidance.* London: Department for Education and Skills. Available to download from www.teachernet.gov.uk/_doc/7767/Transitions.htm

- is the Connexions partnership aware of the incidence of ASD diagnosis within its client group?
- is there partnership working between Connexions, the local autism society and any locally-based projects supporting people with an ASD?
- is the success of the transition monitored?

The national service framework for children, young people and maternity services also sets out expectations around transition, including that transition to adult services for young people is planned and co-ordinated around the needs of each young person[30] and that multi-agency transition planning takes place to improve support for young people with disabilities entering adulthood.[31]

Monitoring transition

Because people with an ASD are most vulnerable at times of transition it is critical that they are monitored and supported during the entire process. Failure to monitor can lead to the failure of a transition. On the subject of monitoring, Government guidelines state that:

> "The Connexions service, through its personal adviser network, where possible, follows the young person through from school to FE/HE/training, continuing to provide advice and liaising with the provider and the local LSC to address any problems which arise in the new environment." [32]

Individual transition plans

People with an ASD have such individual (and sometimes idiosyncratic) needs that the transition plan should aim to record needs and preferences in some detail.

A good transition plan will not make quick assumptions about which service or type of service is to be used. In the case of a complex disability such as ASD, understanding individual needs takes a lot of time and work. Designing an individual package of support to meet those needs (using person-centred planning processes) will take time and effort too, but the outcomes for the individual are likely to be far better than simply 'matching' them to an existing service. As one professional said:

---

[30] Department of Health and Department for Education and Skills (2004). *National service framework for children, young people and maternity services* (standard 4). London: Department of Health

[31] Department of Health and Department for Education and Skills (2004). *National service framework for children, young people and maternity services* (standard 8). London: Department of Health

[32] Department for Education and Skills (2002). *Autistic spectrum disorders: good practice guidance*. London: Department for Education and Skills

"Support for ASD is about putting something constructive in place [which is] meaningful to the person, but not necessarily to staff. If they say 'I really need this', you have to step up to their standard."

It is also crucial that someone takes responsibility for ensuring action points agreed in the transition plan are carried out, and liaises with all the necessary people to make sure the plan is put into effect. An annual transition meeting should take place to monitor progress and agree any new points of action.

Involving young people

The transition process should involve the young person with an ASD, so that they can play as full a role as possible in decision-making. This will often mean preparatory work with the young person, and making sure that meetings take place on terms that are comfortable for the person with an ASD and enable them to communicate in ways which suit them.

Involving the family

Transition planning is likely to be most successful if the family is fully involved. It is important to make sure that the family knows what to expect at meetings. For example, if different housing options are being discussed (eg supported living) make sure the family understands the implications of these options and has a chance to ask questions before the meeting.

Working successfully with families usually means working on their terms – for example, arranging meetings at times and locations which suit them, rather than expecting families to conform to the schedule of the professionals.

In setting up transition meetings, there are a number of considerations to take into account. These include:

- having clear rules for the meeting
- having written timescales which include times for breaks
- making sure there is an agenda
- keeping language clear and simple
- making sure there is a low arousal environment with no (or very little) background noise, uncluttered walls and low-effect lighting
- being clear about what decisions have been made and what will happen next.

A person with an ASD may find it hard to wait until an appropriate time to make comments and may find it useful to make notes until it is their turn to contribute.

When, as part of The National Autistic Society's *make school make sense* campaign, children with an ASD met with the Children's Commissioner for England, Al Aynsley-Green, he commented:

> *"We had to be very careful about not overloading these children with bright colours, with noise...to have quiet space for them to relax in and to be comfortable in. These aren't things that cost large amounts of money. It's a cultural change, it's a way of understanding the lives of these children and how we can improve it for them."*

Advocacy

Advocacy is particularly important at times of transition, to make sure the individual (and their family) is able to communicate their needs and wishes. The local authority should make sure that advocates are available for young people with an ASD if they need them. It should also be made clear whether the advocate is acting on behalf of the young person or the whole family, because as children grow up there may be tensions between the aspirations and wishes of the parents and those of the child.

Securing appropriate adult services for a young man with Asperger syndrome

The case of a young man of 17 with Asperger syndrome and OCD [obsessive compulsive disorder] was referred to Rotherham Advocacy Partnerships by the children's disability service. There were only two weeks until the young man's 18th birthday and he had no adult services to continue the home support he had been receiving. Learning disability services would not accept the referral because they viewed him to be too high-functioning for their service. The mental health team would not carry out an assessment without a letter from the young man's GP. The client's case was passed from one service to another without anyone taking responsibility.

An advocate worked with both the client, finding out about his wishes for the future, and his family and their wishes for service support to continue.

The advocate emailed the managers of the learning disability service and the mental health team to complain and to alert them to the urgency of the case, and negotiated with the children's disability service to extend their support package until a decision had been made.

The client is now getting a service from an occupational therapist from the mental health team, receiving direct payments for home support and looking into independent living.

Community care assessments

For many young people with an ASD, a community care assessment at 18 can be a vital stage in the transition process.

Many families are struggling to cope and, when faced with a further assessment process, may think it easier and simpler to opt out and continue meeting their child's needs largely on their own without support. Some families may be unaware about the importance of the assessment and hence 'opt out' through lack of knowledge. This could possibly apply to families from minority ethnic communities with limited literacy skills, or from socially deprived backgrounds.

As one social worker said, 'If you skip out of the community care assessment you are on your own.' Keeping families engaged with the process is therefore critical.

It is vital that families are aware of the community care assessment process. For example, information days could be held for families. One advantage of identifying and tracking people with an ASD in the school system is that community care assessments can be offered automatically when the person turns 18.

Key recommendations for local authorities

- Ensure you know how many children with an ASD are likely to need services and support once they leave school over the next three to five years. This should include an assessment of their likely level of need.
- Ensure that services that will be needed in three to five years' time are commissioned (based on your assessment of the number of children with an ASD in the school system and their likely needs for housing and support).
- Form a transition planning group specifically for young people with an ASD which includes all professionals relevant to transition planning from school to adult life.
- Ensure that your Learning Disability Partnership Board has a transition champion with knowledge of ASD.
- Ensure that all Connexions personal advisers (and future IAG advisers) working with young people with an ASD have a good understanding of ASDs and their impact.
- Follow the good practice guidance on transition published by the DfES Autism Working Group.
- Ensure that young people with an ASD (and their families) have access to advocacy.
- Ensure that all young people with an ASD, including those without statements, have access to early and effective transition planning and support.

Autism and independence

Person-centred approaches

Does the local authority offer a person-centred approach to planning services for people with an ASD? Does this approach include meeting people's aspirations as well as their needs and fully involve family, friends and advocates?

A person-centred approach is at the heart of *Valuing people*, the learning disability White Paper published by the Department of Health in 2001. In *Valuing people*, a person-centred approach is seen as central to delivering the Government's four key principles: rights, independence, choice and inclusion.

Valuing people requires Learning Disability Partnership Boards to introduce person-centred planning in their local area in order to increase the extent to which services are tailored to meet the needs and wishes of people with learning disabilities, including people with an ASD.

- A person-centred approach involves listening to the person and making sure they are always at the centre of planning and delivery of services.
- A person-centred approach is about creating and offering a life that meets the individual needs and aspirations of people with an ASD – as opposed to matching individuals to services on the basis of availability.

However, person-centred planning is not simply a 'technique' that can be applied using a toolkit. It is a holistic approach that involves looking at the person and their wishes, needs, abilities, goals and essential lifestyle requirements. The appropriate support that each person needs to achieve their goals can then be put in place.

The person-centred plan

As part of a person-centred approach, *Valuing people* requires that each individual should have a person-centred plan.

This plan should be a comprehensive portrait of an individual and what they want to do with their life. It is an opportunity to bring together all the important people in that individual's life – including family, friends, support workers, advocates and other professionals.

Person-centred planning has some things in common with other planning approaches (such as care plans and individual programme plans) but there are important differences too. Person-centred planning:

- starts with what's good about a person and what is important to them
- is based around the social model of disability
- always puts the person in the centre of the process
- emphasises the support required to achieve goals, rather than limiting goals to what an existing service can manage
- doesn't impose limits on what people can achieve, given the right support
- views the family as a key stakeholder in the way that arrangements are made to support the individual
- is based on an explicit set of values, rather than a particular set of questionnaires or tick boxes.

The plan should be treated as a living document and be kept constantly under review.

Recent research into the impact of person-centred planning concluded that it 'had a positive impact on the life experiences of people with learning disabilities'.[33] However, the same research also showed that people on the autism spectrum were less likely to receive a plan than people with learning disabilities. The authors concluded that:

> *"These results, and in particular those relating to mental health and autism, indicate some powerful inequalities in the extent to which people are likely to receive a person-centred plan and, if they do, the level of benefits they can expect."*

The fact that people with an ASD are less likely than people with learning disabilities to receive a person-centred plan is a cause for concern, since it suggests that this group may be missing out on the benefits that person-centred planning can offer.

---

[33] Emerson, E. et al (2005). *Impact of person centred planning*. Lancaster University: Institute of Health Research

Autism itself presents challenges to the person-centred planning process, since many people with an ASD experience difficulties with communication, abstract thinking and expressing their aspirations, all of which are at the heart of person-centred planning processes.

It is therefore vital that local authorities make sure that all people with an ASD are given access to person-centred planning and that, if required, extra support with communication and advocacy from someone who understands ASD is available. It is also essential to work closely with those who know the person well to gain more understanding of what the person may want out of life.

Multi-agency working

A person-centred approach will require people and agencies to work together and be capable of responding to individual needs and aspirations. Support and services accessed by a person with an ASD may include:

- housing options (including alternatives to group homes)
- alternatives to day services which can offer a range of day opportunities, using the community as much as possible
- social groups and other programmes
- social skills training
- employment opportunities – either in supported or open employment, or through volunteering
- an opportunity to access direct payments
- support to enable people to access further and higher education
- advocacy to enable people with an ASD to have their needs and aspirations recognised.

People with an ASD should also have a choice about how and where care is delivered, and by whom.

Local authorities may already offer some of the above to some people, some of the time. However, a person-centred approach is likely to increase demand for these in order to achieve the outcomes required by the person-centred plan. There is likely to be an increased need for the service providers to engage with each other, and with the family of the person involved, so that the individual receives co-ordinated, seamless support.

Improved outcomes through person-centred planning

Person-centred planning has the capacity to acknowledge and plan for individual behaviour, even if this is very idiosyncratic.

Reducing aromas

One woman with an ASD was made deeply anxious by the smells in her neighbourhood, or of other people. She could remain obsessed with a single smell for weeks. The solution (identified in her person-centred plan) was for several fans to be installed in her living room. This made a significant improvement to her quality of life, and the number of fans was slowly reduced over time.

Right home, right location

Harry was not happy sharing a house in Cambridgeshire with three people with whom he had no particular bond. At times he felt intimidated by one of his three housemates.

Staff at the house felt he needed to move away from this environment in order to relieve his recurring anxieties and maximise his potential. A number of care planning days involving the people important to Harry, such as staff, family and friends, were spent drawing up a person-centred plan and service design for where he would like to live. The plan highlighted that Harry wished to live on his own with the 24-hour support of carers and that his perfect location would be a town with a railway station. He loves to travel by train and be within easy access of his parents.

The staff team managed to locate a two-bedroom detached house in a nearby town with a station and a direct route to his family. An advertisement for staff written from Harry's perspective outlining his needs and interests was placed in the local newspapers. This had a huge response and a team has now been recruited to work with Harry using a person-centred plan, as he is about to move into his new home.

In person-centred planning, the family and wider social network is seen as a source of information, ability and imaginative response. The knowledge of family and other significant people can be invaluable in building up a picture of the support needed by an individual to achieve their aspirations. However, the wishes of the person with an ASD should always be paramount.

> **Part of the workforce**
>
> As part of his person-centred plan, Andrew indicated he wanted to do some vocational activities. He was already involved in plenty of social and leisure pursuits (such as walking and cinema trips) but was keen to get a job and become part of a workforce. Andrew lives at an NAS residential service in Manchester and staff approached Tesco, the local supermarket, who agreed that Andrew could do a few hours of volunteering a week at the store, supported by a member of staff. Andrew sees this as a stepping stone to paid employment and wants to wear the uniform and be part of the workforce at Tesco.

The challenges

Although person-centred planning has many merits, there may be some challenges when using this process with people with an ASD.

In particular, staff will need to be trained in ASD and fully understand the impact of ASD on that individual, as well as having a good knowledge of person-centred planning, to take full advantage of a person-centred approach.

The process may also need to be more structured than for people with learning disabilities and take advantage of different ways of communicating. For example, many people with an ASD prefer visual communication rather than verbal. Before embarking on the person-centred planning process it is essential to find out how a person prefers to communicate.

Some people with an ASD will be able to articulate very clearly their desire to, for example, have their own home or move to a new town. However, many people will need a great deal of support to express their needs and wishes.

Many people with an ASD may not understand abstract concepts such as aspirations, dreams or desires. They may find it difficult to imagine or visualise a life other than the one they are already living. Thinking about the future in vague terms may also cause anxiety. Conversely, they may also aspire to be a pilot or to work in the City, but without any understanding about how realistic these goals are, or how to make them happen. Person-centred planning helps people to work towards their goals. Achieving these small steps helps people to develop confidence and self-esteem, rather than a sense of failure.

Meeting very individual needs

Margaret, a woman in her 20s, was not at all happy sharing accommodation with two other individuals with autism and this manifested in challenging and sometimes destructive behaviour.

Staff from The Kingwood Trust adopted a person-centred approach and spent a lot of time encouraging Margaret to communicate through drawing (she is a talented artist), story writing and filmmaking via the use of a camcorder. Margaret can talk but her speech is difficult to understand.

It became clear that Margaret, who has perfect pitch, is extremely hypersensitive to noise and that even a song played in the wrong key would be very painful to her. She also wanted to live in a blue house on her own in a specific Oxfordshire village. Through the use of film she was able to be very specific about her needs and wants.

Through a shared ownership scheme a house was secured for Margaret and within a month of her moving, there was a dramatic improvement in her behaviour. Her staffing ratio has been reduced from as many as three-to-one when out in the community, to one-to-one. Once staff started listening to her, a trust developed, she had more control and, as a result, was much happier.

Person-centred planning can also sometimes feel uncomfortable for parents, since it gives their children the authority to take risks and make their own wishes known, which may not always match the wishes and aspirations of their parents. This can cause tension, especially if the person with an ASD is living at home. Parents may need convincing that their child will not be abandoned or put at risk should they make an unwise decision.

Although many parents go through this unsettling feeling, it can be more pronounced in the case of parents from black and minority ethnic (BME) communities. These parents may feel that service providers or advocates may not understand the importance of their cultural or religious norms and may encourage their children to make decisions contrary to these. It is important to have a good understanding of different cultural expectations in order to provide support to these parents.

It is not uncommon for individuals from BME communities to make decisions which don't match with their parents' thoughts or cultural expectations. Most of them, however, are aware of the consequences of their actions, something which people with an ASD may not be aware of. While encouraging the individual to make their own decisions, advocates have the responsibility to illustrate the impact that these can have on their relations with family and the community.

Conversely, families may also appreciate the sense of involvement that being part of the person-centred planning process gives them. Being able to contribute information about their son's or daughter's early years and having a clearly defined supportive role in the process can be empowering for parents. With appropriate training, families can be excellent facilitators.

The initial plan

Person-centred planning is an ongoing process. However, the initial plan may take between several days and several months to create – this depends on whether it is facilitated by people who know the individual well.

Implementing a person-centred plan will involve not just the immediate service provider but other organisations, agencies and people likely to play a significant role in enabling someone to achieve their aspirations, for example a housing provider, the education service, social services, friends and advocates.

Planning is an ongoing process and all support staff are involved in keeping the plan live.

Person-centred planning tools

How person-centred planning is implemented will vary from person to person. There are a number of structured processes or 'tools' designed to support person-centred planning. Similarly, there are a number of formats for recording someone's plan. Different individuals have developed them in slightly different contexts and they are becoming increasingly well-known in the UK. For more information visit the Valuing People website at www.valuingpeople.gov.uk. The website for person-centred planning in Hampshire may also be useful: www.pcp-in-hampshire.net/

"Person-centred planning…is not simply a collection of new techniques for planning to replace individual programme planning. It is based on a completely different way of seeing and working with people with disabilities, which is fundamentally about sharing power and community inclusion." [34]

Training facilitators

Person-centred planning depends on having trained facilitators who can guide the process. These facilitators should be either the staff, family or friends who are closest to the person. However, it is essential that facilitators are trained so that they:

- understand the theory of ASD
- understand how ASD affects the individual
- can communicate effectively with the individual concerned
- can suggest realistic ways to implement the plan.

It is crucial that all people involved in facilitating and developing person-centred planning suspend their own values in order to develop plans which respond to the person with an ASD. For example, it is easy for people who do not have an ASD to assume that an active social life is desirable whereas it may be precisely what some people with an ASD may choose to avoid. It is important that staff approach the person-centred planning process with the right values and understanding.

Useful information about training facilitators can be found on the Valuing People website at www.valuingpeople.gov.uk

The right leadership

The person-centred planning process is unlikely to be successful without strong leadership from senior management. When person-centred planning is introduced it is possible that staff roles will change. Staff may take on different responsibilities. It can be challenging for staff in traditional services to accept the new ethos. It is therefore important that senior managers acknowledge and support these changes, and make sure staff receive the training they need.

---

[34] Sanderson, H. (2000). *Person-centred planning: key features and approaches*. Available to download from: www.helensandersonassociates.co.uk

"To develop local capacity for change, services will need to invest in leadership in person-centred planning, build the capacity of first line managers to use person-centred thinking and planning, and find effective ways to support facilitators and link learning from planning to organisational change." [35]

Flexible funding systems to support person-centred planning

Over the past 15 years, there has been a move towards giving people more control over their own funding, thereby ensuring that funding is used on what really makes a difference to the person.

Direct payments

In 1997 direct payments were introduced so that recipients could buy services to meet their assessed needs. The way the money can be spent includes:

- employing personal assistants
- contracting with an agency/organisation
- buying equipment
- taking short breaks or accessing respite services.

Direct payments cannot be used to purchase local authority services or equipment or long-term residential care.

In 2001, direct payments also became available to parents and carers of disabled children and 16 and 17-year-olds. However, there is still a relatively low take-up of direct payments among people with learning disabilities. It is not known how many people with an ASD access direct payments, but the figure is likely to be very low.

The Government's intention, set out in the White Paper *Our health, our care, our say*, to extend the availability of direct payments to those currently excluded should help enable more people with an ASD to access a direct payment. However, to meet this aim, local authorities need to take a much more proactive approach to extending the benefits of direct payments to people with an ASD.

[35] Emerson, E. et al (2005). *Impact of person centred planning*. Lancaster University: Institute of Health Research

Individual budgets

Individual budgets bring together separate funds from a variety of agencies including local authority social services; Access to Work; independent living funds; disabled facilities grants and the Supporting People programme. A single sum is allocated to an individual and they can decide how to spend the money.

Individual budgets have already been piloted through the 'In control' pilots for people with learning disabilities and 13 further pilot projects are now being sponsored and evaluated by the Department of Health. It is vital that people with an ASD, and particularly those with complex needs, are included in these pilots.

Individual budgets have the potential to deliver a hugely flexible range of opportunities to people with an ASD, as an alternative to having services provided by the local authority. Nevertheless, we do not yet know how individual budgets can be used to deliver preventative services. Preventative services, if delivered in good time, may decrease the likelihood of an expensive crisis occurring.

If individual budgets are to work for people with an ASD, it will require a range of appropriate services and support for people with an ASD to be available for them to purchase with their budgets. Furthermore, it will also require people who have the expertise to support someone with an ASD to determine how their budget should be used, help them to manage their budget, and ensure that they are not made more vulnerable through this system. The budget also needs to be sufficient for people to be able to purchase appropriate services and support.

Nobody should be 'pushed' to accept a direct payment or individual budget if that is not what they want or if it is not in their interest. Where someone does not have the capacity to make that decision it is important that the local authority should not decide that a direct payment is the best option, in order to avoid providing or developing services to meet identified needs. It is also important that local authorities set the level of a direct payment or individual budget at a realistic level. Sometimes the amount is calculated on the basis of what it costs the local authority to offer an equivalent service in a large, congregate, buildings-based service. This is unlikely to be enough to provide flexible one-to-one support in other settings.

Planning for the future

'We can dream' is a project being undertaken by the Foundation for People with Learning Disabilities in partnership with The National Autistic Society, the London Borough of Waltham Forest and 'In control'. Young people with Asperger syndrome who will be leaving school over the next two years will determine what they want for their future using person-centred planning. They will then develop self-directed supports based on their plans for the future. Young people from mainstream schools and an autism-specific school are involved in the project.

Key recommendations for local authorities

- Ensure that people with an ASD are given equal access to the person-centred planning process.
- Make sure that people have access to an advocate if they wish. The advocate should be trained in the needs of people with an ASD.
- Make sure that staff responsible for implementing and facilitating person-centred planning across the local authority have had training, understand ASD, and are working together effectively.
- Be willing to support the staff from provider organisations whose working roles may change significantly as a result of person-centred planning.
- Find out how people with an ASD prefer to communicate (including exploring non-verbal communication) before embarking on person-centred planning. Adapt planning meetings to take account of their preferred ways of communicating and understanding the world around them.
- Include people with an ASD in individual budget pilots and specifically monitor and evaluate their experiences.

Autism and independence

Housing and support

Can the local authority show that it is taking a strategic approach to meeting the current and future housing and support needs of people with an ASD? Is the local authority committed to finding the right housing solution for each individual?

Housing and support are clearly crucial if people with an ASD and their families are to have greater choice and control over where and how they live, which is one of the stated aims of *Valuing people*.

However, *Tomorrow's big problem: housing options for people with autism* reveals that there is a huge gap between the amount of housing and support currently available for people with an ASD and the demand for it. This is likely to increase in future.

> "In many parts of the country there are serious limitations in the total supply and range of [housing] services available and many have had to move away from their local areas." [36]

The report estimates that a further 8,500 housing places are needed nationally to meet the needs of people with both an ASD and an accompanying learning disability, and that the numbers for those with Asperger syndrome would 'exceed twice this figure'.

It is worth noting that 44% of adults over 25 with an ASD live at home with their parents, rather than in any of the housing options which we detail in this chapter. [37] So for the majority of people with an ASD, 'home' still means the family home. This can lead to problems as parents age and need care themselves. When the parents die, or become too infirm to cope, this often leads to a crisis in the life of the person with an ASD.

Local authorities need to plan to meet levels of future demand and create services which are most likely to meet identified needs.

---

[36] Harker, M. (2004). *Tomorrow's big problem: housing options for people with autism*. London: The National Autistic Society
[37] Broach, S. et al (2003). *Autism: rights in reality*. London: The National Autistic Society

The basis for a good quality of life

For many people with an ASD the outside world feels very unsafe – just coping with daily life can make huge demands on someone's resources. Having their own home (somewhere which is predictable and can be trusted) and appropriate support can help to improve their quality of life.

"The good thing about living on my own is I'm more independent. I'm not so dependent on my mum and dad. I'm able to make my own choices. I'm free to do what I want. The good things about my independence include having a job to go to which gives me a sense of direction. I belong to a church and have friends who live locally."
Person with an ASD

Conversely, getting housing wrong can cause extreme anxiety and stress for people with an ASD. Living in a communal setting, for example, has the potential to be extremely difficult for someone with an ASD. Sharing their space and lives with people they have not chosen (and in situations over which they have limited or no control) can lead to difficulties. Situations that most people would find tolerable can become unbearable to someone with an ASD, for example because of extreme sensory sensitivity. However, for some people communal living can provide a sense of security and community and will be welcomed. Again, each individual will have different needs and it is important that service providers recognise these.

Noise matters
Noise was a real problem for Judy. Her sensory sensitivity meant she was troubled by too much noise, including sounds such as running baths, flushing toilets or pans clattering so far away that they would not trouble most people. She lacked the skill to go to the landlord and explain her problem, so she was trapped in a situation that was causing her extreme anxiety and distress.

Similarly, planning decisions that may appear to make sense in many ways can have unforeseen implications because of the impact of ASD.

Nice house, shame about the location
One excellent housing project in North London had the single drawback of being close to a concert venue. Planners hadn't anticipated that the noise, traffic and crowds on concert days would cause so much anxiety and distress to people with an ASD.

It is therefore essential that those involved in planning understand the impact of ASD when making decisions about the location and nature of the housing services being offered.

Housing options

As with anyone, different people with an ASD wish for and require different types of housing. In time, a change in housing options for them may be necessary as their needs and desires change, for example from the parental home to supported living, or from a larger group home to a smaller group home (and possibly eventually to a place by themselves). With age, their housing needs may also change once again, perhaps taking physical frailties into account, or a wish for a different type of lifestyle. Local authorities will need to ensure that there is a range of housing options to meet the needs of individuals with an ASD.

These may include some of the following, although this is not an exhaustive list.

Self-contained, individual housing
This could be shared ownership, accommodation which is rented – either from a commercial landlord or a registered social landlord (housing association), bought in trust, or through an interest-only mortgage paid through benefits.

Dispersed self-contained housing with support
Where a number of self-contained properties are spread over a single geographical area, with one staff team being shared by people in all the properties. Staff do not live in. Service users can also provide a 'circle of support' for each other.

Self-contained flats within a cluster
Built on one site, including bed-sits and possibly some communal facilities.

Group homes
Two or more people living in the same home and sharing facilities. This is the type of service favoured in the past and therefore, for historical reasons, the reality for many people with an ASD, although many local authorities are now promoting the move to other housing options, such as supported living (see page 62).

Village or intentional communities

A number of people living on one site, often in a rural setting, and forming a distinct community.

Adult placements

Where adults live with a family and become part of that family's life. This is sometimes likened to adoption, although it does not have the same legal implications.

While there is a sizeable body of research on the comparative costs and outcomes of models of supported accommodation for people with learning disabilities in general, there is very little evidence-based research relating specifically to people with an ASD.[38]

Solutions by design

It is now widely accepted that 'some behaviour patterns, compulsions or aversions may be moderated or exacerbated by the design of a house'.[39] Those responsible for planning housing services should make themselves familiar with the ways in which design can create an autism-friendly environment in which people can enjoy living.

If designing a new residential space, it is important to look at how it can be designed **for** autism, so that the building is as autism-friendly as possible.

Generally speaking, buildings should be laid out in a clear, simple way to minimise confusion and create a calming effect. Avoiding long corridors helps to minimise anxiety, and introducing curves, rather than sharp bends, can help to make people feel more secure by removing 'hidden' spaces.

Features such as high-quality sound insulation will benefit people whose sensory profile means that even 'quiet' noises from elsewhere can be very distressing. Homes can also be designed without exposed pipe work, to reduce the risk of injury if people become distressed.

[38] Robertson, J. and Emerson, E. (2006). *A systematic review of the comparative benefits and cost models of providing residential and vocational supports to adults with autistic spectrum disorder*. Lancaster University: The Institute for Health Research

[39] Harker, M. (2004). *Tomorrow's big problem: housing options for people with autism*. London: The National Autistic Society

School designs autism-friendly space

Sunfield School in Worcestershire commissioned architects to build a living environment for children with profound ASD.

The result – two houses incorporating curved corridors, circulation spaces, high ceilings and neutral colours – has produced an aura of calmness and has had a positive effect on the children and the professionals caring for them.

A number of circulation spaces, which are of a size and shape that can be used as play and/or quiet spaces, have given the children more freedom and choice; they can wander around and mix or return to their own space if they want to.

The design itself, with its curved walls and views of the countryside, has instilled a feeling of comfort and security and noise-reducing components such as carpeted areas, high ceilings and natural light have contributed to a calm atmosphere. The use of neutral colours such as grey alongside shades of pink and purple (which have been shown to have a calming effect) has reduced visual stimulation.

The children each have a single room with a low-level window and view to the open countryside. The incorporation of an enclosed outdoor courtyard with covered areas means that children can play independently without being observed by staff.

Planning together

To plan housing and support services for adults, local authorities need to build a picture of likely future demand. The prevalence statistics contained in Professor Gillian Baird's recent report are a good starting point (see page 12 for details).

Planning to meet the future housing and support needs of people with an ASD will require a strong partnership between the local authority housing department, social services, the Supporting People team (where appropriate) and partner providers. It can also be helpful to have a 'link post', someone who acts as a link between these teams.

Valuing people states that each Learning Disability Partnership Board should develop local housing strategies for people with learning disabilities (including people with an ASD), which take account of their personal choices and their person-centred plans.

Local authorities should jointly assess the need for housing and support. This is best done in partnership with users and people who have a detailed understanding of ASD.

It is crucial that this partnership works at senior manager level so that decisions about commissioning services are based on an understanding of potential future needs. Here are some points to consider.

- Is there a forum which allows senior managers from housing and social services to come together to look at how to plan to meet the housing and support needs of people with an ASD? If so, what is the method by which decisions taken at this forum are translated into planning and commissioning decisions?
- Is the local authority aware of the capacity of local providers to deliver services in the future? A strategy to deliver a range of living options will only work if you have providers who are capable and ready to deliver them. Most local authorities now have provider forums – an opportunity for commissioners and providers to plan together.
- Does the local authority have housing managers who are aware that demand for services from people with an ASD is likely to grow in future, and are they planning ways to meet this increased demand?

Supported living

There is a move towards meeting the housing needs of many people with an ASD away from residential settings through supported living arrangements.

Supported living is an approach rather than a single type of service. Indeed, it offers an alternative to thinking in terms of 'service models' into which people with disabilities are expected to slot.

Supported living is an approach based around five key principles.[40]

- Housing and support are offered separately. Someone can change the type of support they receive without having to move house but equally, they can move and still receive the same support. People will have tenancy rights over their own home (eg as home owners, through shared ownership, or as tenants of a housing association or local authority).

---

[40] Kinsella, P. (1993). *Supported living: a new paradigm*. Ipswich: National Development Team

- The focus is on one person at a time and providing a very individual service.
- People are offered a choice about where to live, who to live with, whether to live alone, and who supports them.
- It is accepted that even people with complex or multiple disabilities require choice over where they live and who they live with. Therefore, nobody is rejected from a type of service simply because of the complexity of their disability.
- Existing relationships with family and friends are respected and developed.

Reaching the standard

There is some concern that projects have been labelled 'supported living' in order to qualify for funding, without really offering a supported living quality of service. It is important that all supported living services reach agreed standards, such as the REACH standards put forward by Paradigm (www.paradigm-uk.org). Paradigm's standards outline a way of assessing whether or not a service can be called supported living.

- I choose who I live with
- I choose where I live
- I choose who supports me
- I choose how I am supported
- I choose what happens in my own home
- I have my own home [but don't necessarily own it]
- I make friendships and relationships with people on my terms
- I am supported to be healthy and safe on my terms
- I have the same rights and responsibilities as other citizens.

What type of support?

A range of support options are required to make supported living work, from very intensive two-to-one support for people with complex needs, to a reduced level of support to maintain a tenancy. It is important to remember that people's support needs may also change over time, so the option to move from one form of supported living to another should be available.

Housing is clearly just one important element in a package of 'life support'. Aside from basic care, the range of support needed in supported living arrangements may include:

- emotional support/motivation
- help, as appropriate, with changing accommodation
- budgeting and life skills
- help with benefits
- advocacy and communication support
- access to work and education
- access to social and leisure activities
- help dealing with neighbour disputes
- service user involvement
- health and safety
- property maintenance.

Meeting complex needs

There are a number of projects that demonstrate that people with an ASD and complex needs can also benefit from supported living arrangements. Often this will involve combining funding from social services with other sources (see the 'Flexible funding' section opposite). It is important to spend time understanding exactly how a person's ASD impacts on their daily life, and working out how support can be tailored to meet their needs and wants in a supported living setting.

Supported living meets Annie's complex needs

When Annie first moved to an NAS supported living tenancy, she needed a lot of support from staff with tasks such as washing up and vacuuming. Six years on and she is now dealing with her own finances and doing her own cooking, cleaning and shopping with very little, and sometimes no, help. Her confidence and independence have increased so much that she now feels independent enough to purchase her own home.

Annie holds her own tenancy agreement in Thirsk, North Yorkshire, and support is provided by the NAS. She has a person-centred plan that includes leisure activities and daily tasks such as washing, shopping, dealing with her finances and visiting her care managers and her advocate.

As well as being able to carry out certain tasks and activities more independently, Annie has become increasingly able to make her own decisions

about a variety of things such as what clothes she likes, places she might like to visit and her desires for the future.

She frequently tells staff, her friends and her family that she feels more like an adult and that she loves being more independent. The increase in her confidence and self-esteem is obvious to those working with her. Annie is now in the process of buying her own home in a nearby village and is working with her support team to manage the transition.

Flexible funding

Supported living can be funded from a variety of sources, for example Supporting People, the Independent Living Fund, direct payments or a mortgage with housing benefit assistance.

Funding a supported living arrangement

Two young men with an ASD are living as tenants of North British Housing Association, supported by a care package that includes 24-hour staff support. The rent for the property is £61.60 per week, which is covered by housing benefit. The weekly cost of providing support is £732.38 each. This is funded by the following methods:

Independent Living Fund	£375.00
Social services	£250.00
Client contribution	£ 69.20
Health authority	£ 38.18
TOTAL	**£732.38**

Monitoring levels of support

Whatever housing option is used, it is important to monitor very carefully the levels of support that people are receiving. Even a small change in circumstances (for example, the departure of a familiar warden) can have a profound impact on an individual's quality of life, leading to complications unless someone is on hand to notice and manage the change.

Key recommendations for local authorities

- Make a broad assessment of the future need for housing and support for people with an ASD within the local authority boundaries using the best prevalence figures available.
- Create a joint forum in which housing departments, social services, commissioners and health representatives can together plan future services.
- Make sure that all those involved have training in ASD.
- Create a 'link post': someone who can act as a link between social services and housing departments in order to ensure that people with an ASD have access to appropriate housing options.
- Create a forum of provider organisations to assist in the development of new services.
- Make sure that the model of housing provision offered to someone with an ASD meets their individual needs as outlined in their person-centred plan.
- Make sure that there is a constant review of the level of support for each individual.

Conclusion

This report has discussed how the provision of appropriate services and support can help people with an ASD to achieve a more independent way of life. Living independently can mean different things to different people depending on their level of need. However, giving people with an ASD increased independence of choice cannot be achieved without flexible services and support, and adequate resources to plan and fund these, being in place.

No two people with an ASD are exactly alike, even if their 'level' of disability is the same, nor are their abilities, needs and aspirations. Service planners must be aware of this, and ready to respond to it. This means designing or adapting services to suit individuals – rather than 'matching' an individual to an existing service – and training staff at all levels to understand the particular needs of people with an ASD. Services which have done this report that staff have acquired new skills and become more motivated and confident, and the need for out-of-area placements has reduced. They also report a positive impact on service users, who feel that their views are being taken into consideration and their needs understood: a greater trust has developed between them and the staff, and instances of challenging behaviour have decreased. Person-centred planning has been at the heart of their work.

Person-centred planning should benefit **all** people with a disability, so it is vital that people with an ASD have equal access to the person-centred planning process. Access to advocacy services that have an understanding of ASD, and can help individuals and their families to express their needs and aspirations, will enable them to participate fully in the process.

Planning for adult services should start early so that appropriate provision is put in place now to meet the needs of children and young people coming through the education system. Adult service providers should liaise with children's services and use prevalence rates of people with an ASD in their area to inform their service planning. Help at transition, which many young people with an ASD find an especially anxious time, is crucial to achieve ongoing, seamless support for them as they make the move into adult life.

Autism and independence

There needs to be clarity within local authorities about which person or team will take the lead in supporting adults with an ASD, especially those at the higher-functioning end of the spectrum who often 'fall down the gaps' between learning disability and mental health teams.

We have cited a number of examples of good practice in this report of people with an ASD receiving support that enables them to lead a more independent life. Many of those involved in providing this support have commented on the importance of awareness training for staff and the willingness to work in partnership with other organisations and professionals as well as, crucially, people with an ASD themselves and their families. It is heartening to hear about the positive outcomes this work has had on the lives of people with an ASD. However, it is still only reaching a minority of people with an ASD. There is much to do if all people with an ASD in England are to receive the support they need.

We all have aspirations and wishes and they are often 'ordinary' ones: a home where we like living and feel safe; a job we enjoy; a chance to pursue our interests. People with an ASD may find it more difficult to express these or to realise them, but that does not mean that they want or need them any less. Local authorities have a key role to play in providing services which help people with an ASD to realise their aspirations and to live a fulfilling life with as much independence as possible. We encourage them to act on the recommendations in this report and to promote independence for all adults with an ASD.

Autism and independence